Painting Penguins Green

The Art of Developing a Creative Workforce

Marilyn Rawlings

authorHOUSE™

1663 LIBERTY DRIVE, SUITE 200
BLOOMINGTON, INDIANA 47403
(800) 839-8640
WWW.AUTHORHOUSE.COM

©2006 Marilyn Rawlings. All rights reserved.

No part of this book may be reproduced, stored in a retrieval system, or transmitted by any means without the written permission of the author.

First published by AuthorHouse 3/15/2006

ISBN: 1-4208-8566-9 (sc)

Printed in the United States of America
Bloomington, Indiana

This book is printed on acid-free paper.

TABLE OF CONTENTS

LIVING LIFE OUTSIDE THE BOX..............................1

BUT, MY STAFF IS TOO BUSY TO HAVE FUN....7

ICE BREAKERS 13

BUGS, BUGS AND MORE BUGS..........................17

GETTING DOWN TO BUSINESS 20

DO EMPLOYEE RECOGNITION PROGRAMS WORK?...25

DEALING WITH NEGATIVITY IN THE WORKPLACE...30

WINNING WITH WINDBAGS..............................36

IDENTIFYING YOUR COFFEE STAINS 40

DRIVING UP PROFITS 46

HO, HO, HOLIDAYS? 49

WHEN NOTHING BUT THE BEST WILL DO 53

BARREL, BARREL, WHO HAS THE BARREL?......58

FREEBIES (or almost) !!!..................................64

GIFT CERTIFICATES IDEAS...............................68

CREATIVITY IN MOTION...................................70

IDEAS ONLY FOR THE BRAVE AT HEART 72

LIVING LIFE OUTSIDE THE BOX

"I like nonsense. It wakes up the brain cells. Fantasy is a necessary ingredient in living. It's a way of looking at life through the wrong end of a telescope, which is what I do. And that enables you to laugh at life's realities."
Ted Geisel (aka. Dr. Seuss)
(1904 - 1991)

Every year new buzzwords, acronyms, or phrases appear in the business market. We had Total Quality Management (TQM), Management by Objective (MBO) and many others. They come in and go out like the tide at the beach. A more recent catch phrase is "thinking outside the box." Many people brag that they are "out of the box thinkers." In today's workplace, it's really not enough to have an occasional thought that is outside the box. Many people have built successful companies based on their one unique idea. It doesn't, however, mean anyone would want to work for them. In many of these corporations, the staff is comprised of overworked, antacid chomping, driven employees who are looking for a different place to work. Their organizations are not fun places to work.

What would happen to an organization if the outside the box **thinkers** decided to **live** outside the box, not just go outside for an occasional thought or two? What if their creative juices and thought processes never became dormant? What if the leaders in the organization continually encouraged their staff towards creativity and spontaneity? Imagine a company where creative, talented people were lined up to work for it.

The person who enjoys their work the most, the person most people enjoy working for, is the person who is <u>constantly</u> innovative in his/her thought processes and who serves as a catalyst for others. People enjoy working for an out of the box "dweller".

So how does some one encourage creativity? Is it a natural born talent or ability? Or, is it something that can be learned and developed? Is it simply a choice that one has to make?

While natural creativity in some areas may be an inborn talent, everyone can learn to think creatively. The decision to <u>stay</u> in that creative mode is a choice.

You may feel that your company is in a rut or always strives to play it safe. You may not particularly feel like much of a risk taker. Living outside the box has little to do with risk taking. It has everything to do with thinking differently.

So how do you change the way you think? How can you develop a fresh perspective on the way you do business? There is a great saying that states, "If you always do what you've always done, you'll get what you've always got." (OK the grammar isn't the best, but the sentiment speaks volumes.) If we continue to run our businesses the way we've always run them, nothing will change.

By nature, I am a conservative person. I love reading and learning. I was never a sports minded, physical type. My husband, Wayne, on the other hand, grew up racing cars and riding motorcycles. Two more different types have never existed. After several years of marriage, I realized that maybe I needed something to jolt me out of my comfort zone on both a professional and personal level. I began to think about what I could do that would be totally out of character for me. I decided to learn to ride a motorcycle.

Now for some of you that might not be a stretch, but for me, this was huge. I thought about it, weighed the risks, and listed all the reasons I shouldn't do it. Then I realized that this wasn't something I could "think' through. It was simply something I needed to do. Within a few days, I signed up for the rider's course at the local Harley-Davidson dealership.

The weekend of the course was unseasonably cold for southwest Florida and the 43-degree temperature was all the reason I needed to keep me home. But new thinking requires pushing past your excuses. Four days and several bruises later, I came home with my motorcycle license. I was thrilled! I had accomplished something that I never dreamed possible. I had pushed my body and my thinking way beyond what I thought was possible for me.

And now, when I want to clear my head or come up with a new way of looking at a problem, I get on my motorcycle (yes I bought one of my own) and take a ride. On days when I know I have to be creative and innovative, I even ride the motorcycle to and from work. Riding that bike reminds me that I can do anything I set my mind to do.

What is there that you could do that would be a stretch for you and your thinking? It may not be taking a motorcycle course. For you, it might be taking a Spanish class at the local community college, reading a book from beginning to end or learning to play the banjo. Make the decision today to do something you never thought you would (or could) do and then take the first few steps to make it happen.

So, now that you are taking your first steps toward changing your organization, how do you get your staff to go along for the ride? Like any other change you want to initiate, you must take it slowly and introduce the changes a little at a time.

For us, the changes started quite by accident. One day I had a craving for Cappuccino. Not the expensive $5.00 per cup kind from a fancy coffee bistro but rather the cheap syrupy kind from a machine at the local convenience store. I think it's made with a touch of coffee and A LOT of sugar. I decided to stop and pick up a cup on my way to the office. I also purchased an additional cup for one of my staff members who loves cappuccino.

Upon arriving at the office, however, I realized that the person I bought the cappuccino for was on vacation that day. Now what should I do? If I gave the coffee to one staff member over another, I could ruffle some feathers. How would I choose?

Then the idea came. I went to our facility's paging system and loudly announced, "The first employee to come to the front office and tell Marilyn how nice she looks today, gets a free cup of cappuccino." I put down the microphone and waited, wondering if anyone would actually respond. Within minutes, several employees rushed the front office each declaring the virtues of what I was wearing that day. I gave away my extra cappuccino to an employee who wasn't even sure he liked cappuccino. The competition, not the cappuccino, had made him run like a mad man to the front office.

Several hours later I found out that my little competition had sparked quite a bit of conversation throughout the facility. The usual negativity and complaining had taken a temporary turn to new horizons. I knew I had something here. This book outlines a journey from a boring team to one alive with creativity. Your organization may be somewhere in between but you too can begin "Painting Penguins Green."

BUT, MY STAFF IS TOO BUSY TO HAVE FUN...

"Timing has a lot to do with the success of a rain dance."
                                                                          - Unknown

When we first implemented our "fun" times, I was concerned that people would think we were goofing around all the time and not getting any work done. I was concerned that my staff would think I was crazy. My concerns were endless. I have to admit, I was nervous. Yet through this journey, I have learned two things...timing and timing.

One important first step was to learn to "read" my staff and the office environment. No matter what you attempt to implement, no matter what you try to do to have fun in the office, if you try something at a time when your staff is under incredible pressure to get a job done, your plan (no matter how inspired or creative) will fail miserably. Think about how much you enjoy interruptions when you're trying to get an important task done under a tight deadline. Your creative juices are flowing and someone stops by to chat. It can be frustrating.

I have also learned that when my staff is stressed, I might think they need a diversion to lighten things up a bit. They, however, may just want to be left alone. It's a fine line, but one you learn to walk as you get to know your staff and their temperaments.

In order for "fun" to be successful, you must learn to read your staff. For some, fun can help to relieve stress. For others, fun only adds to their stress. Know which ones are which.

PICKING AND CHOOSING YOUR TIMES

The end of each fiscal year is an incredibly hectic and potentially overwhelming time for my staff. Nerves can get raw and tempers can flare. Last year, I knew they were stressed to the maximum. We had just had to fire one employee so they were not only handling year-end pressures, they were also picking up the slack of being one person short. Each staff member was coming in early and staying late. On several occasions, they had to be reminded to go home at the end of the day. (How many bosses would love to have that problem?)

I could tell, however, that because of the excessive workloads, emotions were running on overload and tempers were short. That would NOT have been a great time to interrupt the workflow or to try to do something funny. I might think they needed it even more at that time but it wouldn't have been appreciated.

However, several weeks after the crunch time was over and a new person had been hired, I knew the time was right. So, I hired a massage therapist to come to our office. She set up a massage chair in our conference room and I offered each of the 8 members of my leadership team a 15-minute chair massage. It was optional, of course, but not one team member turned it down. They loved it. (They have suggested I provide this service on a weekly basis!)

If you think you can't afford to do something like this, check to see if your company will help foot the bill. If not, then come up with something similar to help them unwind. Give them an afternoon off with the "condition" that they must do something to relax. For some, that may mean catching up on errands they haven't been able to do because of the late night hours at the office. For others, relaxing might be an afternoon fishing or walking on the beach. For another, it may be a walk through the mall (retail therapy).

If an afternoon off isn't possible, send them home an hour or two early. If they use the excuse "I have too much to do to take the afternoon off," remind them that the work will be there tomorrow. If they don't take the time off to relax today, they may not be healthy enough to finish the work tomorrow.

Do whatever is within your authority (and pocketbook) to do. Remember that some of your ideas might even be tax deductible!!

IF YOU ACT NOW, YOU COULD WIN A WONDERFUL PRIZE...

One of the perks of being a supervisor is attending regional and national conferences. Many of these conferences are accompanied by trade shows featuring vendors hawking their wares whether office equipment, software, cars, or services of some kind. Most of these vendors also offer give-aways from pencils to Frisbees to bobble-head dolls. Most supervisors return home with a huge bag of these free goodies. Usually these "trinkets" collect dust and are eventually forgotten or thrown away.

But what if you could use them to get "points" with your employees? My trade show giveaways have become the basis for a prize box. This prize box is used to provide rewards for many of the ideas in this book and contains pens, t-shirts, pocket knives, hats among other things. Most of the items were obtained for free at trade shows. The remaining items were marketing items donated by local vendors.

A good friend of mine uses all the items he collects at trade shows to stuff mini-Christmas stockings and then he gives them to his employees. This will let your employees know you think about them when you're away.

ICE BREAKERS

"Sometimes when I get up in the morning, I feel very peculiar. I feel like I've just got to bite a cat! I feel like if I don't bite a cat before sundown, I'll go crazy! But then I just take a deep breath and forget about it. That's what is known as real maturity."
- Snoopy

Every organization goes through transition times of some kind. These awkward times may be as a result of new leadership or changes of major policies or procedures. Many times, these awkward times are the result of employees that have not come together. The people all work together but they are not a team. There is little real communication. Ideas are hidden, not shared. People are competitive and self-seeking, not cooperative. While it's relatively easy to train someone to do a job, it is much more difficult to teach people to overcome learned attitudes and perceptions.

The ideas in this chapter can help move your team to a whole new level. Instead of gathering in groups to complain, employees will have something new to discuss.

EMPLOYEE TRIVIA CONTEST

Often, as your organization grows and new people come on board, it is difficult for people to get to know each other. They are separated by fears as well as cubicle walls.

At staff meeting one day, we asked everyone to write down their name and a little known fact, some personal bit of trivia, something that no one else in the organization would know about them. We received everything from "I was asked to audition for Second City Television" to "I collect model trains."

At our next staff meeting, we distributed a list of all the little known facts. We set up the list like the "matching" test from elementary school with employee names on one side and the bit of trivia on the other. We asked the employees to try to match the fact with the staff member. They would have two weeks to try to figure what secret belonged to which employee.

For the next few weeks, the work place was buzzing with chatter about dreams and secrets. A great deal of time was spent trying to get to know one another and guess whose secret was whose.

Several weeks later, we unveiled our "secret identities" to the group and the person with the most correct answers won a small prize (from the prize box of course).

For those of you who wonder how to break into having fun in your office, this is a great way to do it. It is also a non-threatening way to help build your team and to bring them together for a common purpose.

BABY PICTURE CONTEST

This is not particularly a new idea but one that still works. Simply ask everyone to bring in a baby picture, place them on a sheet of poster board or bulletin board and ask everyone to try to figure out who's who. Again, this is a great icebreaker for a new team of employees. Help them to get to know something about each other. Give them something new and productive to "talk about around the water cooler." Of course the one who guesses the most correctly wins a prize.

CUTEST KNEES CONTEST

This is a great alternative to the baby picture contest. Ask for volunteers that are willing to have their knees photographed. Have them roll up their pant legs and shoot the pictures. Simply post the photos on a poster board and number them accordingly. Give everyone a chance to guess who's who.

We used this idea as a fundraiser for a local non-profit group. Each vote cost $1.00 and the money raised was given to the charity. The person who identified the most knees correctly won a prize donated by a local vendor.

BUGS, BUGS AND MORE BUGS

"You can discover more about a person in an hour of play than in a year of conversation."
- Plato (427 BC - 347 BC)

Living in Southwest Florida has some wonderful benefits...75 degrees in March is just one of many. I was not prepared, however, for the incredible number (and types) of bugs that permeate the Florida landscape (and often the workplace). It is not uncommon to see large "Palmetto Bugs" (up north they would be called cockroaches) crawling around homes and offices. Pest control businesses make a killing (literally) in Florida.

One day, one of my staff members let out a scream as a large Palmetto bug carried her desk half way across the office. People came from all over to see what the ruckus was. Another idea was born.

That weekend we purchased several packets of "bug" stickers from a local card store. They were large and creepy looking just like the Kamikaze cockroach that threatened our office earlier in the week. We carefully numbered each sticker.

Early Monday morning, I casually walked throughout the work place planting the bug stickers on items throughout the facility. Bugs were stuck to oil cans, calculators, and desks. You name it. It had a sticker. I quietly jotted down the number and location of each bug. The plan was in motion.

On Tuesday, at the close of our all staff meeting, I announced to the staff that "bugs" were hidden throughout the facility. Some bugs were quite obvious. Some were more carefully hidden. All were visible to the naked eye. Nothing had to be moved. The staff's job was to simply find the bugs and bring them still attached to its source. When they did, they would be able to choose a prize from my secret stash.

Within the hour, grown men and women came to my office carrying every thing from 55 gallon oil drums to clocks off the wall in order to claim their prizes.

You may wonder what kind of great prizes would lure adults to participate in such foolishness. The prizes ranged from racing posters to hats and t-shirts. All were giveaways donated by local vendors. You would have thought I was giving away a week's stay at Waikiki Beach. One employee wanted to keep her bugs on the bulletin board in her cubicle (kind of notches on a gunslinger's gun!) so people would know how many she had located.

The Art of Developing a Creative Workforce

Helpful Hint: Make sure you keep a list of where you hide the stickers (I learned this the hard way!) and then remove them from the object when it's brought to you to prevent any duplication.

(check the ice breakers
section for more ideas)

GETTING DOWN TO BUSINESS

"Never does a man portray his character more vividly than his proclaiming the character of another."
- Sir Winston Churchill (1874 – 1965)
British Statesman

BUSINESS CARDS

Everyone in our organization has his/her own business cards. Why? First and foremost, the cards make the employee feel special. Many of the employees had never had business cards of their own.

The cards include the agency name, address, phone and fax numbers, all the "normal" stuff, but no titles. Why? Well, the answer is two fold: 1.) If the employee is promoted, we don't have to buy them new business cards; and 2.) there's no "classifying" of people by title.

If you must include a title, make it one that really fits the job. Exactly what does an "Administrative Assistant" do? That title tells people very little. What if the title on the card was "Customer Service Diva?" Now that's some one a customer would want to help them with a problem.

Most commonly, business cards are used to give to people we meet so they have a record of who we are and how to contact us. In our organization, they have two additional purposes.

First, we use the cards to claim ownership of projects. For example, our vehicle mechanics leave them on the dash of each vehicle they repair. It's their way of "claiming ownership" of the work they do. When their name is attached, they tend to do a better job.

Secondly, we use them as note cards to encourage one another. When one employee sees another doing something special or helpful, they use their business card to leave a note of thanks or recognition. If they see someone who appears "down", they leave him/her a note of encouragement on the back of the business card. It's short and to the point, but very effective. Obviously, the notes can't be lengthy on a 2" X 3" piece of cardboard, but it is usually just enough to make the other person's day. It's also fun to watch the other person's expression when they find a note from a co-worker.

BUSINESS CARDS (again...)

As the team leader, you may often want to say thanks to an employee or tell them what a great job they are doing, but just don't seem to find the time or the opportunity. Weeks go by without saying anything and then it seems too late. Business cards are a great way for the leader to recognize an employee for doing something special. A quick, 30-second thank you note on the back of a business card can do wonders. Leave it at their work area while they are at break or at lunch. When they return, the note is there to greet them.

SPEAKING OF THANK YOU NOTES...

I love getting mail. I'm talking about regular, paper mail, not e-mail. I love the feeling of finding a handwritten note in my mailbox, something other than bills. My mom always made us write thank you notes as kids. It was not an option. I didn't like it but I now appreciate what I learned, the importance of making people feel special and appreciated. We always had to send notes to friends for birthday and Christmas presents.

Think how you would feel to receive a handwritten note from your boss thanking you for doing a great job. I have to admit, in all my years of working, I've only had one boss ever do that. I've had bosses say "good job" as they walked past me in the hallway. There was nothing meaningful about that! I never really even thought they were sincere.

But Don, my note-writing boss, was different. One morning, I was sorting through my mail and I found a handwritten, personalized note encouraging me and thanking me for all my hard work. The note wasn't long but I knew he appreciated my hard work. He mentioned <u>specific</u> things I had done that he had noticed.

Over ten years, the notes continued, thanks for positive publicity about the company, magazine articles, all sorts of things. They were short and to the point but what a boost to my morale! These notes were his way of telling me I was doing a good job and that he took the time to, not only notice, but to let me know he noticed. How hard would I work for him? The sky was the limit.

What made it even more special was that he wasn't my immediate supervisor. He was the CEO of the company several levels above me on the food chain.

Everyone needs recognition. You may even think, "My boss would never do that!" That may be the case but why don't you be the boss who does? Trust me. Your staff will notice.

As the leader of your organization or work unit, it's often difficult to notice what your staff is doing. We do, however, find the time and opportunity to notice the things they do <u>wrong</u>. We even find the time to point out their faults all under the guise of helping them become better employees. Take the time to notice them and more importantly, take the time to thank them.

So let's take this idea and expand it one more level. Let's say that one of your employees has been spending a lot of nights and weekends working on a project. How would that employee feel if you sent a note to his/her mate, significant other or entire family thanking them for the sacrifice they made for the company? How would they react to a note thanking <u>them</u> for their "sacrifice" to make your business a success? Include a gift certificate for a local restaurant in the note if your company policy allows. If necessary, ask a local vendor to donate one. You'll get lots of points with the employee and with the family. Plus, the employee will get points with the family because they all get a night out on the town. Everyone wins!

DO EMPLOYEE RECOGNITION PROGRAMS WORK?

"This is a test. This is only a test. Had it been an actual job, you would have received raises, promotions, and other signs of appreciation."
— Unknown

Many people question the validity of employee recognition programs such as Employee of the Month, Outstanding Sales Associate, etc. claiming they are not effective or at least they lose their effectiveness over a period of time. Yet some organizations have had an employee of the month program for decades and it's equally as important as the day they started it.

When we decided to implement the program, we wanted to have clear-cut guidelines and requirements. Our dilemma was that our work place was very diverse in its job tasks. We had clerical staff, managers, technical people as well as mechanical types. How could we design a program to encompass all the different type of work?

First, we had to find the areas of commonality. What were the employee traits that were the most important to us? What mattered most? First and foremost, it was important that the customer was given the best service and the most accurate information possible. Secondly, it was important that other team members felt they could depend on ach other.

As a result, we came up with the following criteria for our employee of the month program:
1. *Perfect attendance* – In order to qualify, the employee has to have worked every possible day of the month, no vacation time, no sick time. This immediately whittles down the field of eligible employees to a manageable size. It also may help to motivate the person who suffers from chronic absenteeism. One employee, who did an excellent, overall job for me, asked me why she never was named "Employee of the Month." I assured her that I was very pleased with her work and really wanted to give her the award but I couldn't, as she never met the perfect attendance part of the criteria. I explained to her that over the past year, she had not worked one entire month without taking a day off. She didn't even realize how much time she was taking off. I shared with her that I felt her position was critical to the success of the team and we needed her here.

After demonstrating consistency for several months, she was presented with the award. This also helped me to identify a problem we had with her supervisor. While the supervisor and I had discussed the employee's absenteeism at length, the supervisor had never discussed it with the employee. Two problems were solved with one meeting.

2. *Tasks completed under allotted times* – whether the job description is administrative, clerical or technical, there are usually industry standards (or just common sense) for how long a job should take to complete. For example, if a major project needs to be completed by the 20th of the month but the employee finishes it a week early, then he/she would be eligible. If your office staff is required to answer the telephone in three rings, but the telephone continually rings unanswered, then those employees would be eliminated for consideration that month. Industry standards can often provide guidelines for technical and mechanical tasks and help to determine the employee's eligibility requirements.

3. *100% customer satisfaction* – When we started this program, we received very little customer praise. To be honest, we just weren't that good. We realized that we had not established a "praise-worthy"

environment. As we became a more efficient, customer-driven organization, we noticed the change in our customers. Also, we began complimenting our customers and each other. As a result, everyone began to reciprocate.

4. *Overall efficiency or "Doing it right the first time"* - One of my employees seemed to rush through tasks just to get them off her desk and on to someone else's. Often, items were not checked for accuracy and were passed on with incorrect information. This cost the organization countless hours of employee time to re-do reports and explain errors to customers. (If your staff doesn't have time to do things correctly, they certainly don't have time to do them over.) We not only have this criteria in our "Employee of the Month" program, we include it in our employee evaluations. We have found that employees who know they are evaluated on whether or not they (or anyone else) have had to re-do any of their assigned tasks, will slow down and take their time to check and double check their work.

For our technical staff, a repair that requires an additional service call for the same problem within 30 days would fall into this category. (Supervisors make the final determination on whether or not it is truly a re-work of the same problem.)

For office staff, it would mean no errors in correspondence or no errors in reports for the month.

5. *Positive attitude* – This section will allow you to identify and recognize those employees who exhibit a great attitude, those who add value to their teammates and to your organization. Often times, these employees are also the ones who do well in the customer satisfaction area.

In order for this program to work, you need to customize the program to fit your work place. Get a group of your key staff and ask them what characteristics are the most important to them. Then develop the program around those criteria.

If you have a small staff, you may need to make this an "Employee of the Quarter" program. Whatever you implement, make sure that standards set are fair and that everyone has input into the nominee.

DEALING WITH NEGATIVITY IN THE WORKPLACE

"It's so much easier to suggest solutions when you don't know too much about the problem."
- Malcolm Forbes (1919 - 1990)
Publisher

Negativity can be one of the most destructive forces in the workplace. How does the leader of an organization deal with it? A constant barrage of criticism from some employees, if allowed to ferment, can undermine even the greatest leader and the greatest customer service.

My number two, and right hand person, is a man named Danny. He is a trusted employee, friend and, if all goes according to my plan, eventually my successor.

When I arrived as the new leader of the organization, I was warned about Danny. He had been promoted by my predecessor to a supervisor position, a move that many employees had questioned. He was known as a "pot stirrer" who helped to keep the rumor mill in motion. As my staff got to know me, they questioned whether or not Danny would last.

Negative employees seem to enjoy monitoring everyone else's work habits and continuously offer "suggestions" on how others should do their jobs. They may even discuss their suggestions with co-workers under the guise of "trying to help." As a result, they can come across as critical and a bit self-serving. If the other people in the organization don't implement their suggestions, they become frustrated and share how under-appreciated they are or how poor of a job their supervisor is doing. Many times, however, these employees simply are bored with their jobs and find other people's jobs more interesting than their own.

This was the situation with Danny. He had been a mechanic for years. He knew that something was wrong with the way the facility was being run. He just didn't know exactly what or how to fix it. When he became one of the main supervisors in the organization, he had the chance to make a difference. The problem was he was the newest and the youngest of three team leaders.

Shortly after Danny's promotion, one of the other three supervisors decided to retire. Because money was tight, we decided not to fill his position and allowed the remaining two to split his responsibilities. They did a great job but Danny was the shyer of the two and took a back seat to the other man.

About a year later, the second man decided to accept a job at another facility. We were in better financial shape now so financially we could afford to replace him. I asked Danny what type of person he thought we needed to hire and how he thought we should split the responsibilities. To my surprise, Danny said he didn't think we needed to replace his co-worker at all. He had a plan to change the way things were being handled and that we could save some money in the process.

While I knew Danny was bright, I was concerned that he would be stretched too thin. He presented some of his ideas to change the way he ran his section of the business. They sounded plausible so we decided to give a few of them a try. After several months with Danny at the helm, his area was running more smoothly and more efficiently than it had in years. My "pot stirrer" had simply been a frustrated employee with a great deal of untapped potential.

Simply changing a problem employee's areas of responsibility can make huge difference and give them something new to do. Giving the employee a more challenging task can change their point of view of the organization. At a minimum, they will begin to see the rest of the organizational pie and not just their little slice of it.

The Art of Developing a Creative Workforce

There are employees who are simply negative people, not creative and not necessarily bright. It's up to the leader to discover which is which and then to be willing to let the truly negative ones "search the possibilities of the outside job market."

So how do you tell the difference? Often it's just your leadership discernment that must kick into action.

We tried something a bit unusual to test the waters in our organization: employee switch days. In the past, when a program was not successful, the employees blamed each other. "I would have had my part done but Charlie didn't order everything I needed to complete the job in time." Charlie claimed that the other employee hadn't told him everything he needed to order. The blame went on and on.

The switch days simply moved some of the employees to another job for a period of time (usually only 4 – 8 hours). This time would help them see the facility from another person's point of view.

Prior to the actual switch days, I asked all employees to choose three other areas of interest within the company. There were no limits, no restricted areas. Even my job as Director was fair game. (Your organization may handle highly confidential information where you might not be able to open up access to some areas.)

Then we reviewed the list and wherever we could, we gave the employee their first choice. Then once a week for three weeks, we allowed one third of the staff to work with someone else in the organization for the day. Of course, I tried to place the people who were most critical of the accounting department with one of the fiscal staff. People who constantly criticized our warehouse people were placed there to handle irate customers, internal staff and incessantly ringing telephones.

So what did this do for our organization? First, the critical employees learned exactly what the subject of their criticism went through on a day-to-day basis. One employee, who had been extremely critical of our warehouse area, exclaimed "I'll never be critical of them again. I had phones ringing off the hook and crabby customers. It was terrible." He realized that on many occasions, he had been one of those crabby customers.

Secondly, the program brought a new set of eyes into essential areas of the organization that offered genuine ways to improve how they do business. For example, our warehouse manager worked in an area that utilized the warehouse more than any other. Logistically, that part of the operation was at the far end of the building. It just didn't make sense to have them that far away. Workers who only occasionally needed items from the warehouse were 20 steps away.

Because of major equipment located in their area, we couldn't re-locate the entire department to be closer to the warehouse. The warehouse manager could however, bring part of the warehouse to them. As a result of his switch day, he set up a large cabinet in their area that housed the most commonly needed items from the warehouse. They were presented with a written inventory and each week they counted and re-stocked it. Both areas were winners. The warehouse manager reduced the traffic at his warehouse counter and the workers saved time formerly spent walking from one end of the facility to the other.

WINNING WITH WINDBAGS

"Before I came here I was confused about this subject. Having listened to your lecture, I am still confused. But on a higher level."
- Enrico Fermi (1901 – 1954)
Italian – American Physicist

Have you ever been in a meeting that dragged on well past the time that it should have taken? People in the meeting droned on and on, even after their point was made. Why does that happen? Why do thirty minute meetings take 90 minutes?

One Fortune 500 company decided that all their meetings would be held in a conference room without chairs. All the participants stood the entire meeting. As legs became tired, discussions became briefer. For them, it worked. While the standing staff meeting may not be conducive to your organization, there are some things that can be done to speed them up.

First, the reasons for the lengthy meetings need to be identified. Most meetings will take at least as long as they are scheduled to take. If you don't need an hour, don't schedule an hour.

Secondly, is there one person who consistently and inappropriately monopolizes the discussions? Is there one person who talks incessantly? Does anyone leave at the end of the meeting frustrated because they didn't get the opportunity to share their ideas? By identifying the problem areas, the team leader can begin to correct the problem.

One day our leadership team was meeting with some employees from another department to work on a project. One of the outside team members droned on endlessly trying to make a point and convince everyone that his idea was the way to proceed. Instead of convincing everyone, he alienated almost everyone in the room by dragging the meeting on and re-stating his position over and over. One person even said, "Enough already. We get your point." After the meeting, one of my staff jokingly said, "I wish we had been able to "gong" him." We laughed at his suggestion, but we all agreed.

Of course, the employee's comment referred to the old television show where performers sang (often quite badly) in an attempt to see how long the judges could endure the tortuous ordeal. When the judge had had enough, he/she would slowly rise from his place, pick up a large mallet and hit a loud gong, ending the horrible performance. The audience would show their agreement by applauding loudly. The judge would tell the performer honestly why he had gonged them. Then the performer would be escorted off stage.

My staff member's casual comment planted the seed for yet another idea. The staff talked about Mr. Boring and the gong idea for days until one member decided to do something about it. He cut out a piece of wood for the base, found a metal disc and built a gong. While it is not as large as the one used on the original television show, it is just the perfect size for the center of our 12-foot conference table. A stick with a small round ball serves as the mallet. It is definitely not as melodious as the original but the point is made.

Now, when new comers arrive at one of our meetings, they invariably ask, "What's the gong for?" We quickly explain how the gong came into existence and its purpose in our meetings. We explain that anyone who discusses a point beyond where the meeting participants feel it needs to go can be "gonged" and that anyone in the meeting has the right to gong anyone else. In fact, we encourage the new comer to pick up the mallet and try it out just to see how it feels and what the gong sounds like.

The use of the gong cannot be indiscriminate. Once the gong sounds, the person with the mallet explains why they used it and what they felt the speaker did to turn off the rest of the group. If the rest of the attendees agree, the speaker must discontinue trying to make their point. If they disagree, the speaker is allowed to continue.

So, can feelings be hurt? Can tempers flare? Sure if this idea isn't handled correctly. Everyone knows prior to the meeting that they must present their ideas quickly and succinctly. They must make their point and move on. As a result, most do. We've only had to use the gong a few times. Somehow, just the thought of someone using it, seems to keep speakers brief and to the point.

IDENTIFYING YOUR COFFEE STAINS

"Only the mediocre are always at their best."
- Jean Giraudoux (1882 – 1944)
Diplomat and Writer

Every organization wants to be <u>known</u> for its great customer service but unfortunately, very few organizations want to do what it takes to actually <u>give</u> great customer service. They become so concerned with processing customers that they forget to serve them.

Have you ever been squeezed into one of those narrow airplane seats and tried to read while your knees are pressed up against your chin? The flight attendants move up and down the aisle with their beverage cart bumping into passenger shoulders and legs as they go. As they approach your row, you listen to the beverage choices and make your decision so you'll be ready when they arrive. In anticipation, you reach up to unlatch the seat tray in front of you. As the tray drops down, pretzel crumbs fall in your lap and a dried coffee ring on the tray reminds you of the thirteen passengers who used that tray since it was cleaned last. Suddenly the thought of your little bag of pretzels touching that dirty tray becomes rather disconcerting. Aren't they supposed to clean those trays after each flight? Maybe they're trying to save some money by only cleaning the trays after every other flight?

Where else they are trying to save money. If the airline can't <u>clean</u> their planes, how good can they be at maintaining them?

As business owners, we all have "coffee stains" somewhere in our organizations. We all have areas where we have had to cut back in order to improve our bottom-line. But how have those cut backs affected our customers' perceptions of our business? Is the trade-off worth it?

About twenty years ago, on one of my speaking trips, I went to Tulsa Oklahoma. While in town, I visited a local department store. I immediately was impressed with the selection of merchandise, the cleanliness and appearance of the store and the customer service even though I could find similar, less expensive items at any one of the discounted retail chains. Unfortunately, the department store chain did not have stores in my area of Florida.

Several years later, our local mall expanded and to my surprise, this chain opened a store in our mall. Needless to say, I shopped there often and my check register backed this up. Eventually I opened a charge account with them and many of the sales people recognized me at least by sight. Some even knew me by name. They watched items they knew I wanted and called me when they went on sale. If I needed an item in another size and they didn't have it, they called a nearby store.

Lately, however, this store has changed. It's different. I'm sure that the changing economy has affected them just like everyone else. Recently, I had some time to kill while waiting for my children to finish basketball practice. I ran to the mall to see what I could find. I entered this store as I had so many times but something was different. The store didn't look different. The product quality was seemingly the same. I walked from rack to rack but NO ONE spoke to me. I walked past one clerk who never looked up from papers she was shuffling and past another who was writing something at her check out counter. Another stood at the register and watched me pass by without even acknowledging my presence.

What had happened to my beloved store? Where was the feeling of "specialness" that I had felt before? Finally I found one of the sales clerks that had helped me in the past. I asked her to page the manager. I explained to the manager that I had been a loyal customer for over fifteen years and that I was disappointed that no one had spoken to me in over 30 minutes in her store. She explained that "sometimes that happens" and she would "review the security tapes" from my visit. You can imagine that gave me a warm, fuzzy feeling. Needless to say, I left disappointed.

I didn't give up and several weeks later came back for another visit. This time I found a jacket I really liked but unfortunately not in my size. No problem. I knew that the employees at this store would call to one of their other store and find it for me. After spending the next five minutes trying to locate someone who could help me, I finally found a woman moving clothes from one rack to another. I asked if she could help me locate the size I needed. Without looking up, she said, "no, that's marked down 50%. We can't call on anything marked down more than 33% or we get in trouble."

I quickly scanned what I could see of the huge department store and saw one other customer way down at the other end. Obviously, her reluctance to call wasn't because she was too busy waiting on other customers!

Fear of a reprimand kept her from going the extra mile to serve a customer. Excellent customer service had become a victim of policy and procedure.

What procedures do you have in place that limit your staff from giving the "WOW" customer service moments that your customers want and your competitors will fear?

IDENTIFYING YOUR WOW MOMENTS

We've all heard stories about companies who have gone above and beyond to give their customers extraordinary service. The stories usually involve employees assisting a pregnant woman giving birth on a bus, CPR administered to a person having a heart attack or some other exceptional medical condition.

But how would their "normal" customer service compare to these occasional stellar moments? How do they treat the people who visit their company on a regular basis? Are their customers excited about dealing with them?

So, how do you get started providing your customers with "WOW" moments? A great place to start is by asking your customers what services they would like you to offer. I'm not talking about some impersonal customer survey sent in the mail. Most people don't (or won't) take the time to fill them out anyway. Personally, I resent being asked to give a good evaluation so the employee can get a raise, promotion or more commission. Treat me great and I'll give you a great evaluation. Sounds fair to me!

Why not spend some time in your primary customer areas or waiting room talking to your customers? Ask them if they were greeted cheerfully? Were they dealt with promptly and courteously? Was their request/concern handled completely? What would they change about their experience with your company?

One company's CEO decided to randomly chat with people as they waited in the company's waiting area. Each person was asked how they were treated, what they would change, and what suggestions they had to improve the company. As a result of the customer's suggestions, the CEO had a computer installed in the waiting room so clients could check e-mails and communicate with their offices while waiting. He also added several newspaper subscriptions for his clients to read and keep up on their areas of interest. These were simple (and relatively inexpensive) changes for the company but were "WOW" moments for the customers.

Secondly, ask your employees where they think you should improve. Give your employees the opportunity to identify the "coffee rings" in your organization. For every real "stain" they identify, give them a gift certificate to Starbucks or another local coffee shop.

Recently, I visited a vehicle maintenance shop and saw a great slogan posted on the wall. It read, "If we're not customer driven, our vehicles won't be either." That says it all.

DRIVING UP PROFITS

"Nothing is really work unless you would rather be doing something else."
- Sir James M. Barrie (1860 – 1937)
Playwright

In many companies, sales representatives and certain administrative staff are given a company car to use. The selected vehicle usually meets some pre-determined criteria set by the company's fleet department. In most cases, the size of the vehicle is in direct proportion to the employee's position on the corporate ladder.

What if lower level employees had the chance to drive a bigger car, one with more "status" in the company? Would the sales force be motivated by the chance to drive a Lincoln Town Car (or similar luxury vehicle) for the month? If the money just isn't there to make that happen, maybe one winner could be chosen from the top 10 producers or the top 10% of your sales force. The name of each person who qualifies could be written on a separate piece of paper and randomly drawn from a "hat" at a sales meeting with a large percentage of the sales force in attendance. Those who qualify should be in attendance whenever possible to help build up the excitement for the next month's drawing. It can also help prevent any naysayers from claiming the drawing was "fixed" or the winner pre-determined. Make it a big event!

Still can't afford it? Why not ask your local, luxury car dealer to "donate" the use of the car (or at least offer it at a reduced rate) in exchange for some free publicity? They may not be willing to donate the vehicle for the entire year but they might be able to handle the donation for one or two months. Find five or six vendors who are each willing to donate for two or three months and your year is covered. Still skeptical? See if you can talk a car rental agency into donating a luxury vehicle for one evening! The employee could go out to dinner and travel in style.

You may want to check with a local limousine company. They might donate a limo for the evening in exchange for the balance of your company's limousine business. You're a non-profit group and don't have limo business? Better yet, you can offer the vendor a tax deduction for donating their services.

Providing coverage of the event by the local news media is a great way to show the vendor that there is something in it for his/her business too. You may want to "publicize" the award by utilizing a magnetic sign on the side of the vehicle. For example, the sign could read,

"The driver of this Jones Ford vehicle was Acme Tool Company's top sales person last month."

If the dealer is still hesitant, try bartering services with them. What does your company have to offer that the dealer might need? Does your organization have an exceptional training program? Would the dealer's employees benefit from attending some of the training sessions your company offers? Remember, thinking creatively can often determine the success of an idea!

What about the employees who don't even have the use of a company vehicle? They may not need to be rewarded with a luxury vehicle, but what if the Employee of the Month was offered the opportunity to use a company car for a week or even a month? Make sure the rules for their usage of the company vehicle are in line with company policy and more importantly, the same as for other employees in order to maintain the integrity of the program.

HO, HO, HOLIDAYS?

"In everyone's life, at some time, our inner fire goes out. It is then burst into flame by an encounter with another human being. We should all be thankful for those people who rekindle the inner spirit."
- Dr. Albert Schweitzer (1875 - 1965)
Missionary

Holiday parties, either in the office or at an alternate site, are standard fare for most offices. Some are well attended. Others are not.

About 15 people, including spouses and significant others, attended our first Christmas party. I was so disappointed. No one had wanted to attend. I guess I couldn't blame them too much. We weren't a team by a long shot. We were simply people who happened to work in the same facility.

Policy prohibited us from paying for the party with company funds, so each employee had to pay for their own meals. What conversation took place was forced and strained. Even I didn't have a very good time.

So how were we going to get more employees to attend? What incentive was there to attend a party with people they didn't really know and then pay for it themselves. First, we tried the altruistic approach and asked everyone who attended to bring a toy for an underprivileged child. (Let's see...during everyone's busiest time of the year, we asked them to pay for their meal and their mate's meal PLUS buy a gift for someone they didn't know...and we wondered why that didn't work?)

The next year we changed to a food drive. Needless to say, that didn't work well either. Nothing seemed to help. Obviously, the organization was not ready to attend a party for just humanitarian reasons. We needed motivation.

We were one of those companies whose policy prevents employees from accepting gifts from vendors. It's a great policy...keeps people honest. But in spite of our company's rules, vendors still sent cheese baskets, gift certificates and all sorts of gifts. The problem? What should we do with them? Most couldn't be returned. Again, an idea was born.

Now, each year when we receive gifts from vendors, we put them into our Christmas "gift box" for giving as door prizes at our Christmas party. Prizes are awarded randomly by pulling names and numbers out of a "hat." Each employee is guaranteed to win a prize. Suddenly, the employees had a reason to attend. They were still asked to pay about $20-25 per person to cover the cost of the meal and the room. But, they were also guaranteed to get at least half of that back in prizes or gift certificates. There now was "something in it for them."

Some may think that it's sad to have to "bribe" your employees to attend. I prefer to think of it as "creative marketing." Within several years our attendance at our parties increased from 20% of the employees to over 90%. Now, ten years later, we still give out door prizes but along with that we successfully collect toys and canned goods for local charities. The conversation is lively, and we all have a great time getting to know each other better. We now live what we could only picture years before. We have begun to look outside ourselves.

Most recently, we decided to adopt a local needy family and provide Christmas for them. We talked about it as a group and envisioned the delighted little children rummaging through piles of packages and wrapping paper. We contacted a local social services agency and they gave us the names and ages of the members of a family in great financial need. In spite of everything, we were disappointed to learn that that the little children we pictured were actually teenagers! What would we do? The employees collected gifts, wrapped them and prepared them for delivery. One person even donated a tree with all the lights.

Several weeks went by and we received a call from the mother of the family. She had a special request. Would we mind taking some of the money we collected and buy presents for a young mother and her three little children? She didn't mind if she didn't get anything but she hated to see the little ones go without any presents. Here was a woman in need who saw someone else whose need was greater.

The employees jumped in to help. When other departments in our organization heard what we were doing, they started buying presents too. Needless to say, both houses were filled with gifts on Christmas morning. We truly had come full circle.

WHEN NOTHING BUT THE BEST WILL DO

"If a man does his best, what else is there?"
- George S. Patton (1885-1945)
U.S. General

So what do you do when your team really pulls off something great? The project is under-budget, on time, and really brings some positive attention to your organization or company. In a large corporation, a cash bonus may be an option. But, if you're in a small company, government agency, or non-profit organization, your options may be more limited.

This is when your creativity needs to step up a notch. How can you reward employees without being able to attach a financial reward? Many times, organizations make the mistake of always rewarding employees with money. While money is not bad, it just can't become routine or expected. By keeping your staff off balance when it comes to the reward, they will be more prone to think creatively.

(If the reward must be cash, try to make it in the form of a bonus, not a pay increase. Pay increases will increase your overall budget and annual recurring costs. A bonus is a one time operating expense.)

Let's say an employee does an exceptional job on a project. You want to reward him/her. So, you give the employee a small cash bonus of $100. Of course, the employee is excited to get it. After all, every little bit helps. They arrive home and tell their family about the bonus. Before they can take off their jacket, the family has the money spent. The kids want new CD's. The electric bill needs to be paid. Before the next day of work, the money is gone.

So, what are your options?

TAKE ME OUT TO THE BALL GAME

My staff works hard. They really are the best group of people I have ever worked with. Our area of Florida is blessed to have two professional, major league baseball teams, the Minnesota Twins and the Boston Red Sox, and both teams hold spring training in our area.

One day, I was talking to several other employees who mentioned wanting to take a day off to enjoy a spring training game. Suddenly I was transported back to my childhood days in Detroit when we would attend baseball games at Tiger Stadium. I could smell the hot dogs and the popcorn. I could hear the vendors yelling, "Red Hots! Get your Red Hots!"

The voice of one of my employees jolted me back to reality. I realized how nice it had

The Art of Developing a Creative Workforce

been to daydream about the game and enjoy the memories. Another idea was born.

Since one of the stadiums was a County owned facility, I called the people in charge of the stadium and asked how much for 26 tickets. He told me the usual price and then promised to see what he could do. Several days later, he told me I could have them for free if I took my employees to games over three or four different days. He couldn't get all the tickets for the same game.

It was perfect. I could take 1/3 of my staff each day and still provide coverage for the office. But, how would I choose who was to go first?

I decided to look over the names of the last 6 or 7 Employees of the Month (look in the Employee of the Month section for the details of the program) and they would be my first group. I called them all together and told them we were going on a "field trip" the following afternoon. I told them to dress comfortably, bring sunscreen and some money for lunch. I had prefaced this meeting with talk in a prior all staff meeting about "giving back to the community." It had been an unintentional set up. They immediately pictured themselves on some kind of road crew clean-up program. It was perfect.

About noon the next day, a dejected and apprehensive group of employees gathered in the front office. They weren't quite sure what this was all about, but they were pretty convinced they wouldn't enjoy it. We loaded everyone in a large van and slowly drove away from the facility. After about ½ mile of driving, we stopped the van in the middle of the road and opened all the doors. They just knew this was where they were going to start their road crew "clean-up." Instead, I handed them each a ticket for that afternoon's Minnesota Twins game. They were dumbfounded. I thanked each of them for their contribution to the team and said this was my way of saying thanks. All I asked in return was that they make up an appropriately horrifying story to tell those employees who remained behind in the shop and who would attend a game the next day.

When we returned several hours later, they shared stories of backbreaking labor and the hot sun with the rest of the staff. Of course, it was all a set-up. They were a bit "pink" from sitting in the sun, so it only made their story more credible.

The next day, when I met "team two" in the front offices to prepare them for the field trip, I wondered if team one had been able to carry off the hoax. When I saw one employee with latex gloves hanging from his back pocket (guess he didn't want to touch the garbage with his bare hands), I knew they had been successful. By the time the third group went, a few knew the truth but overall very few knew where we were really going.

It's been two years since our outing to the ballpark. Yet when I ask the staff what one "weird" thing that we've done was the best, it's an almost unanimous decision, the day at the ballpark.

You may not have a baseball stadium near by but you have something special to offer even if you are in a small town. Do you have a local restaurant whose specialty is home made pie? Ask the vendor to donate a piece of pie and a cup of coffee to your staff. Another vendor may donate gift certificates for a movie and popcorn. The choices are endless.

If possible, and office coverage/company policy will allow, actually take them to the restaurant for a much needed break. Give them time off from work to go see the movie. Ask the local newspaper or television station to cover their accomplishments and the vendor's part in the plan. The media's involvement provides great incentive for the vendor to donate his/her product and great recognition for your staff. A group photo in the local paper or on TV may be just the thank you they need to know how much you appreciate them.

BARREL, BARREL, WHO HAS THE BARREL?

"Those who can laugh without cause have either found the true meaning of happiness or have gone stark raving mad."
- *Norm Papernick*

Hopefully, by the time you're reading this chapter, you have begun to generate some fun ideas of your own. Hopefully you have tried some of the ideas in this book and made them work for you and your organization. But how do you know when your organization is ready to implement some of the really wild ideas you've come up with? Most of the beginning ideas can be implemented right away. Others must be based on the climate of your organization. If your staff needs to get to know each other better, implement some of the relational ideas. If you need to improve your holiday celebrations, choose the holiday ideas.

Starting the process of "Painting Penguins Green" will at times be thoughtfully carried out and implemented. Others will just happen. Moving further along in the process, however, will need to transition along with your organization and the people in it. As your organization develops, the unusual things you do will develop also.

For the really bizarre or unusual things you do, you will have to trust your instincts. The ideas in this chapter developed for us over time. Don't try to rush your staff to this point. Allow things to develop naturally. Remember this should be a "crock potted" process, not a microwaved one. Give it time to develop slowly. The ideas at this stage must be implemented in an environment built on trust and friendship. If not, they will fail miserably.

One of my staff members, Randy, is very creative. He can make anything out of a piece of metal or a piece of wood. For this idea, Randy was given the task to make a Fleet "barrel". I didn't tell him what it was for. I only gave him some general guidelines about the size and the color. The barrel was to be about 24-36 inches in height and very colorful. After that, he was on his own to be as creative as he would like to be.

Several days later, he returned to my office with a very unusual looking apparatus. The lower part was made from the base of an old (and emptied) fire extinguisher which he had filled with metal ball bearings. He then attached about 18 inches of a broom handle to the neck of the extinguisher. Afterwards, he covered it with brightly colored paint and reflective tape. The fleet "barrel" Randy made was probably one of the ugliest things I had ever seen. It was perfect!

As staff arrived at our next all-staff meeting, the barrel, in all its glory, was waiting for them, prominently displayed in the middle of the conference room table. I purposely was not in the room as I didn't want to answer any questions about the barrel's presence. Randy was there but even he didn't know its intended purpose.

We proceeded with our normal staff meeting with the usual discussion and presentations. At the end of the staff meeting, we presented our Employee of the Month award, something we had been doing for many years. In my opinion, however, the award was becoming routine and stale. It was losing its punch. So when the Employee of the Month was announced, I asked the employee to come up to the front of the room. I always shake his/her hand and give them their certificate. This time however, there was a twist.

Along with the usual recognition, I announced that the winner would be the recipient of this beautiful "barrel." The winner looked at me skeptically suggesting that perhaps someone else should win the "award." Then I explained.

Each month, the Employee of the Month will be presented with the barrel and given 24 hours to hide it somewhere within the confines of the building. The only requirement is that some part of it be visible to the naked eye at a normal standing height. The job of the rest of the employees? To find where the barrel is hidden. Once found, the "finder" will have 12 hours to re-hide it, again with the same restrictions. If no one can find it after a few days, any staff member can ask for a "barrel location verification." This simply means that the person who hid it last must tell me where it is so I can verify that the hiding place meets all the criteria.

At first, the barrel was placed in rather obvious hiding places, behind a desk, up on a shelf. Over time, the employees became more creative in their hiding places. Some stayed late at night to hide the barrel when others weren't around. But as their ability to hide the barrel increased, so did the creativity of those searching for the whereabouts of the barrel. Some came in while it was dark and used a flashlight to hunt for the barrel. Why? Because the barrel had reflective tape on it and the beam from the flashlight would cause the barrel to glow in the dark! Espionage became rampant in the organization and alliances formed. Employees were talking about little else.

The goal? To be the person in control of the barrel at the time of the next month's staff meeting and to present it to the next Employee of the Month.

The reward for possession of the barrel? A trip to the prize box of course.

Several months into the barrel competition, we began remodeling the administrative offices. As I worked at my desk, a solemn faced, construction worker came into my office. Calmly he stated that we needed to evacuate the building immediately. He explained that when removing some ceiling tiles, he had located a strange looking "canister" up in the ceiling with only the tip showing below the tiles. He was concerned that it was a bomb. I smiled and asked if it was rather strange looking with weird colors. He responded, "Yes."

I then had to explain to him that he had just found the fleet barrel and he now had 12 hours to hide it somewhere in the facility.

What makes people want to participate in something like this?? It certainly isn't the baseball hats and pens that are in the prize box.

First and foremost, people were created to be competitive and curious by nature. A game like the fleet barrel will allow your staff to be both. Secondly, it allows them to have fun and be creative at work. Giving them a project to start their creative juices flowing will encourage them to look at every thing they do in a whole new light.

FREEBIES (or almost) !!!

Most bosses would love to give their employees something extra for doing a great job. The problem for most is finding the money to pay for the program. There's nothing in the budget, and no money to do what they would like to do for them.

There is hope however. Listed below are a bunch of ideas that are really inexpensive to implement. In fact, most of them are free.

1. Allow the employee to leave a couple of hours early on Friday afternoon and arrive an hour or two late Monday morning;
2. Have the boss or company CEO take the employee out to lunch (just the two of them);
3. Give them the use a parking place close to the building;
4. Reserve a parking place for the "Employee of the Month";
5. Send the employee a personalized thank you note (for a job well done) to their home via the US mail;
6. Send the employee a personalized E-thank you;

The Art of Developing a Creative Workforce

7. Use the back of your business card to write a quick thank you to leave under their car's windshield wiper; (Make sure rain is not scheduled!)
8. Talk to local government about donating a free admission or free parking pass to their parks/pools for a month;
9. Funny gag gifts – crown, tiara for "King/Queen for the Day";
10. Shortened work day for a week (6 or 7 hour workdays instead of eight);
11. Invite the employee to your home for dinner or bring them lunch for a day or week;
12. Ask local businesses to donate inexpensive advertising products (Sport Caps, ice scrapers, rulers, etc.) to give spontaneously to employees who exhibit great customer service;
13. Ask your local animal shelter to waive the adoption fee for a puppy or a kitten (make sure the employee is really interested!!);
14. Recognition of the employee's accomplishments in the Company or departmental newsletter;
15. Recognition at the Company's executive Board meeting (in person);
16. Hat or Shirt with "L.O.T" embroidered on it – "Leader of Tomorrow";

17. Send a Press Release to the local newspaper regarding the employee's accomplishments (great coverage of the Company's achievements too!);
18. Honorary Department Director / CEO for the Day;
19. Coupons for "time off";
20. Gold Medal winner – randomly selected from staff nominees; wears "gold medal" around neck all day/week;
21. Day off to spend however they want (Beach, shopping etc.) – not charged against accrued vacation time;
22. Stop for ice cream at local ice cream shop (boss' treat);
23. Comedy day/ Movie Day (employees can watch a movie in the conference room during lunch hour – continue to next day if necessary– include popcorn, soda, etc.)
24. Put employee achievements (Photos too!) on Company's web pages – out of town relatives can see their accomplishments;
25. Choice of Job Title for the Day;
26. Five Minutes of Fame on local governmental cable TV program;
27. Newspaper Ad in local newspaper – include the employee's photo with the words "Job Well Done"; include description of what the employee accomplished as money allows;

28. Have their co-workers serenade them;
29. Let the employee wear jeans to work for a week;
30. Magnetic sign for their company vehicle or personal vehicle for the month;
31. Employee Recognition on bulletin board in lobby of company to showcase outstanding employees;
32. "Employee of the Month" Flag for top of cubicle;
33. Recognition Letter from Company CEO – letter read at staff meeting and copied to personnel file;
34. Boss washes employee's car at lunch time;

If these ideas are not enough, get your employee's juices flowing at your next staff meeting. Simply, divide them into small groups (no more than four or five). Then give them ten minutes to list as many ideas for employee recognition as they can. The only catch is that each idea must be able to be implemented for less than $25. Of course, there should be a prize for the most creative team!

GIFT CERTIFICATES IDEAS

These are great rewards or doing a good job. Check with local restaurants, service providers, car mechanics, movie rental stores, etc. for donations.

1. Tank of Gas;
2. Oil Change;
3. Free coffee at coffee specialty store;
4. Makeover at department store cosmetic counter;
5. Movie tickets;
6. Dinner for Two;
7. Team reward – 15 minutes in a massage therapist's chair (at the office);
8. Local store Gift Card;
9. Subscription to Local Magazine or newspaper;
10. Water Cruise on local ship;
11. Home Improvement Store;
12. Local theme park (Six Flags, Busch Gardens, etc.);
13. Comedy Club;
14. Wal-Mart;
15. Local Grocery Store;

16. One Hour jet ski /Kayak rental;
17. One day ski lift pass;
18. Health Spa / Day Spa;
19. Dinner theatre;
20. Mystery Theatre;
21. Miniature Golf;
22. Local Concert;
23. Car detailing;

CREATIVITY IN MOTION

1. KUDOS Box – Much like the old "Complaint Box" but instead used to collect positive comments about employees; the comments are read to co-workers at staff meeting or listed in the department/company newsletter;
2. Flowers for the employee hand delivered by the CEO;
3. Plant for the employee's office;
4. $25 Calling Card;
5. Game tickets for a local sports team – to be attended during work day;
6. CHOCOLATE!!
7. Catered lunch (from boss and served by boss) for employee and one guest;
8. Corporate apparel;
9. CD player with headphones;
10. Flashing star pins – for stellar customer service;
11. Cookie Bouquet – to match the theme of the project;
12. Personalized stationery – "From the desk of _____"; "Words of Wisdom from _____";
13. Everyone in office must call the employee "Sir" or Ma'am" for the

week/month; If they don't, they put a nickel in a pot; Money goes to employee (or favorite charity) at end of week/month;

14. "Sticky" $20 Bill to slap on employee's back;
15. "Hall of Fame" wall for employee accomplishments;
16. Traveling trophy that gets passed around to employees as they accomplish good things;
17. License plate frame – "I was _(Company Name)_ 's Employee of the Month";
18. Motivational/leadership type books/tapes;
19. Unique name plate for cubicle or desk that stands out from the rest;
20. Employees of the Month Luncheon - all dept. winners get to attend luncheon with some of the CEO's of the company – each receives a specially designed "Employee of Month" T-shirt;
21. Hat/Shirt/ Bumper sticker with "I did the Right Thing" on it;

IDEAS ONLY FOR THE BRAVE AT HEART

1. Have other staff serenade the employee with a personalized song written just for them.

2. Arrange for the employee of the month/year to ride the Zamboni at the hockey game;

3. Arrange for the employee to throw out the first ball at a baseball game;

4. Give the employee a "Get out of _ _____ free" card – gets them out of a boring meeting or otherwise unpleasant/menial task;

5. Sit in the dugout / VIP seat at a local sporting event;

6. Autograph session with players from one of the above teams;

7. Surprise recognition in front of the crowd at a local sporting event;

8. "Mall-a-thon" – have stores donate prizes and person follows "clues" from store to store in search of the prizes;

9. The Barrel - hidden throughout building - employees work to find it - person who has it at end of month gets prize;

10. Put employee's photo /accomplishment on the side of a local transit bus;

MY EMPLOYEE'S CREATIVE IDEAS:

Use this page to list the creative ideas generated by your employees. (Remember, submit your idea to us for inclusion in the next edition of "Painting Penguins Green." If selected, you and your company will be featured as a creative organization.)

1.

2.

3.

4.

5.

6.

7.

8.

9.

10.

11.

12.

13.

14.

15.

16.

AND IN CONCLUSION...

Several important tips to remember;

1. Start your program slowly;
   Remember the analogy of the crock pot vs. the microwave.

2. Allow it to develop naturally (don't force it);
   You can't force people to have fun and have a good time at work. Don't try. Most will see others having a good time and want to join in. Others will never get with the program. Enjoy the ones who do and don't let the others get to you.

3. Have fun doing it;
   The idea should bring a smile to your face. If it doesn't, the idea probably won't work for others. Run the idea past somebody else if you need to. If you are one of the people who has a hard time having fun, find someone else in your organization who is better suited to the task. While I think it works best if it comes from the top, something is better than no fun at all.

4. When an idea has run it's course, let it go. When interest in the barrel began to wane, I tried to talk it up and keep it

going. Month after month it became a chore for me to monitor its whereabouts and find out who hid it last. The idea had been so successful, I just couldn't face letting it go. Now the barrel sits on the credenza in my office. Visitors still ask about the strange apparatus and I have the opportunity to tell the story all over again. Keep the memories alive but don't dwell in the past.

* * THE BEGINNING * *

If you have a "barrel" type experience that you would like to share, send your story to Marilyn Rawlings at:
> Xchange
> PO Box 938
> Ft. Myers, Florida 33902

OR

E-mail it to:

Marilyn@xchange-online.com

Who knows? It may be included in our next edition of "Painting Penguins Green."

ABOUT THE AUTHOR

Marilyn Rawlings is a dynamic speaker whose energy and passion has transformed work places and leaders throughout the country. She is a much sought after keynote presenter and has spoken to diverse audiences from governments to universities and private industry.

Marilyn is known for her humorous, yet professional, presentation style that instantly connects with her audiences. As a long-time, successful leader of a multi-million dollar organization, Marilyn not only talks the talk, she has learned to live it.

As someone who loves to help people reach their full potential, she is passionate about her message and able to communicate it with intensity, excitement and humor. Marilyn has written articles for various magazines, newspapers and trade journals regarding her successes in the business community.